GREENF.
MADE EASY

A Guide to Greenhouse Growing

Author: Simon Marlow

Published by: SANDSPublishing

Copyright © SP&SK Enterprises, LLC

First printed December 2012, 2nd Edition

ISBN-13:978-1475067507

ISBN-10:147506750X

CREATED & PRINTED IN THE UNITED STATES OF AMERICA, DISTRIBUTED WORLDWIDE.

Other Titles by SandSPublishing

Easy Growing Container Gardens

Easy Growing - The Plant Growers Handbook

Make Solar & Geothermal Work for You

Grow Marijuana Weed Indoor or Outdoor

This Page Left Intentionally Blank

Use it for Note Taking

Table of Content

This Page Left Intentionally Blank

Use it for Note Taking

PREFACE

The need to eat to survive is endemic in all of us should we wish to grow and prosper and since 'we are what we eat' then isn't it time we review what in fact we eat. Many of us today have such busy schedules that we have lost the art of eating what is good for us rather than what is provided to us as in the way of fast foods. The abundance of processed foods makes it easy for us to be fully nourished but mostly over-nourished. Most processed or industrial foods are grain, corn and soybean based. So if this fact is true and we are what we eat then this makes us mainly 'corn'! This is the likely single factor that makes many in the western world overweight, that and lack of sensible exercise. Putting exercise aside for the moment then we should consider the factor what we eat with some concern. Whether you eat fast foods, or even make your own meals with purchased products it comes down to the fact that you just don't know what you are exactly eating! Meats are mostly fed on grains, vegetables are sprayed with insecticides, fertilizers, hormones etc and both meat and vegetables maybe genetically engineered to grow faster and resist infection. So in essence what this all comes down to is that you don't really know what you are eating and so you don't really know who you are!

With the surge in interest in organic food (organic vegetables and organic meat - still not fully sure what this means) and the growing concern over food supply and quality many are now taking to growing their own food whether that be vegetables, chickens, goats or whatever. Many of us do not have the luxury of growing our own meat however you will be amazed how easy it is to grow both vegetables and flowers (often used to control insects) all year round and in limited space by using the modern day greenhouse.

This is the topic of my book on greenhouse growing, I explain the basic concepts of the green house and some of the more popular types such as cold frames, lean-tos etc. But added to that I explain in simple terms how to grow from seed, how to select the appropriate soil and how to select a greenhouse to meet both your financial restrictions and your growing desires. I have included many of the most valuable on-line sites that provide much more in-depth reading; however this small book will provide all the information you need to start growing your own plants, whether they are flowers, herbs, vegetables or even plants for your yard or garden.

I have spent the last 20 years growing most of my own plants and have thoroughly enjoyed the experience. I have even invented a system that allows me to plant and grow without any further intervention other than harvesting, so vacations are no longer suicidal for my plants!

Finally I know that growing your own does not cover all that we eat, but it is a start and this beginning can be inexpensive and fun just to see what you can do. I believe the art of growing must be maintained by us all to reduce the effects of industrial foods and life changing events such as wars, global warming and other unexpected catastrophes that may affect our food supply.

To this effect this simple book provides all in one place the aspects of greenhouse growing, from selection, building, operating and growing. It provides many additional key resources of the best of the best on-line websites that provide much more advanced in-depth reading to allow you to grow not just simple plants but also exotic plants from the tropics. So don't wait read on and quickly learn the basics of 'Greenhouse Growing Made Easy'.

This Page Left Intentionally Blank

Use it for Note Taking

INTRODUCTION

Chapter1: Greenhouse Growing a Hobby for Life

Build a hobby or business that will last and create a unique experience that you can share with others. Grow your food all year round and feel good about knowing where your food comes from. Also grow your own plants and colorful flowers

Chapter 2: Greenhouse Basics

All you need to know about the various types of greenhouse environments so that you can select the best type to meet your budget and to grow the plants you desire

Chapter 3: Greenhouse Types

Positioning your greenhouse is essential to create one of the three types; Hot, Warm and Cool greenhouses. In this chapter I show you how to decide which greenhouse is best for you.

Chapter 4: Greenhouse - Placement, Tools and Materials

Greenhouses come in four basic structures: Glass, PVC, Plastic and Polycarbonate structures. Different structures are best suited to different climatic areas.

Chapter 5: Greenhouse Growing Guidelines

This chapter delves into organizing your greenhouse to allow you to grow various types of plants letting you know the 'How and Where' to plant in your greenhouse

Chapter 6: Greenhouse Plant Soil Guidelines

Getting the right soil type is essential for your plants. Find out about soil fertility and texture. Get to know about soil types and understand how to balance soil pH using the soils own electrical currents. Find out how to put it all together to maximize your potential for unrelenting success.

Chapter 7: Greenhouse Watering and Water Conservation

This chapter focuses on water a key element for success in growing. I show you ways to save water both in the greenhouse and outside through automation and drip feeding into pots and compost bags.   Now expand these techniques to your whole garden.

Chapter 8 Bring Life to Your Greenhouse

Now that you have a successful greenhouse how can you extend it and use it all year round. This chapter shows ways to grow all sorts of wonderful plants. Make your vegetable and flowers last through the year.   Sell your excess plants to cover all your costs.   Freeze the rest for winter snacks and those days you just need comfort food.

Chapter 9: Greenhouse Lovers / Hobbyists Additional Resources

A great resource page for finding additional information at your finger tips. Online/offline places for more cool information about greenhouses

Chapter 10: Checklist for Buying a Greenhouse

Depending on your decision buy the greenhouse that makes most sense for you. Follow a simple checklist, this chapter shows you how.

Chapter 11: Concluding Thoughts

How the benefits of greenhouses exclusively the rich and famous of yester year are now available to all. There really is no stopping you from growing, making anything in harmony with the planet.

Extend Your Knowledge

Additional resources using a unique watering system from growing plants directly from compost bags:

References

Additional related books to help you grow more efficiently

CHAPTER 1: GREENHOUSE GROWING A HOBBY FOR LIFE

Ask yourself this question: Why do I need to grow anything? I can purchase what I need when I need it, so why bother? Very simply, there is a biological need I believe, in everyone to create something unique and different. Growing provides that unique creativity because every plant is unique in its own biological right which means that you can create your own unique experience. Added to that pleasure, is the real benefit of knowing you have grown the plant from seed or sapling.

I have been growing just about everything for the last twenty years in spaces not larger than a 3ft by 3ft window sill to a garden or yard that is 50 ft by 50 ft. I've grown plants in greenhouses, under a glass 'lean-to' and growing directly outside. I've grown vegetables, flowers, bushes, trees, evergreens and so on. I have the satisfaction of seeing the results of my labor and in many cases some plants will still be around when I'm long gone. For me that helps me understand a part of my existence and legacy.

Particularly for me now, I have a real concern about the food we eat, not only from a pesticide perspective but also about the energy required to transport food from the farthest corners of our planet when all we need do is grow it locally. Take for example garlic. What drives me nuts is garlic shipped from

China. The cost, in terms of emissions alone, simply makes this ridiculous and even reckless Garlic can be just about grown anywhere. Why would anyone in their right mind grow garlic in China and then ship it around the world to countries that can easily grow garlic?

In today's uncertain life in the sphere of what we eat and drink, growing your own plants can give you that certainty of what you consume. Growing plants for food can be extremely enjoyable if you simply follow a few rules of gardening. Plants like humans require a lot of attention at certain stages in growth and this is where most people fail. In general either plants wither and die from neglect (no watering), from being overwatered or compost/soil that is poor quality. This can be managed through a system I use to automate just about the whole process of growing which will be described later in this book.

There are many advantages to growing plants whether vegetables, flowers, shrubs and saplings in a greenhouse. The nice thing about growing plants in a greenhouse is that you will have complete control over how you protect your precious plants, although you won't necessarily be weed and pest free just because you are growing indoors. Also growing indoors like this will give you a head start as your plants will be protected from the extremes of weather

This book brings together all the facts and data you need to be successful in growing both in your greenhouse and then into your yard or garden. It starts with selecting and purchasing your own greenhouse to construction and then on to operation.

This book leaves no stone unturned when it comes to gardening. It provides you with soil type data that best suite certain types of plants. It shows you step by step how to grow in the greenhouse and then to transplant outside. It further identifies many plants and how they should be planted.

It also describes a system that you can readily automate the process of watering and feeding whilst removing all the back breaking work of weeding. With this system the only hard work is the harvesting which in most people's book is the best part of growing.

So grow plants, flowers, vegetables or whatever and enjoy the fact that you are the creator and nurturer of your own magical garden. Take delight in what you can create and begin the journey of self-sustenance in a time when dependency on others

Today growing can be extended just about all year round in a controlled temperature environment called greenhouses. This has spurred the greenhouse industry to explode in profits. The need to grow your own fresh food has fired the imagination of many to start down the road of growing their own. Not only does this give you the ability to manage your own food source but it also is a great hobby for later in life giving you somewhat independence from excessive prices in staple foods.

The trend in greenhouse growing started simply in the late 70s but is now a huge growth industry driven by both entrepreneurs in the farming industry and by the small homeowner. This trend has become a top priority for many businesses and homeowners resulting in many types and construction material for greenhouses. This has also spurred the accessory industry for green houses resulting in a plethora of options now freely available for any greenhouse owner.

Greenhouses are to a degree an extension of our personalities; it mirrors what we want from life. And what we want is a steady supply of home-grown healthy organic food. During these times of uncertainty when terrorism and climate change can cast us in the dark for possible long periods of time, we have one thing we can be sure, our food supply to the kitchen will tide us over should the country go into emergency mode. The home grown produce from our greenhouses will be around to feed our families for a few weeks before things return to normal.

So if greenhouses can save our way of life we may at some point in time consider the idea of building one, a first step towards self-sufficiency or independence.

The drive back to locally grown foods are attributed to two key factors; local health and the impact of global warming through reducing transport environment costs. Most greenhouse owners are familiar with the advantages of growing their own plants and flowers, prolonging the growing season and selling the excess fresh produce in the communities they live in. It's not just a constant supply of healthy food that concerns individuals but a greenhouse and building it can become pure enjoyment and clean fun for everyone in the family.

There are many greenhouse models and accessories to choose from. Costs can go from affordable to very expensive. You can build a greenhouse on a budget by using a simple frame with a plastic film stretched over this rudimentary structure to an elaborate metal and glass pre-manufactured sun rooms or arboretum.

Each of them serves the fundamental function of extending the growing season. The trick to making greenhouse gardening easy is watering, watering the exact amount at the right time. This problem has been solved with the use if drip tape and automated battery operated water timers.

My advice if you are a growing novice starting a greenhouse should be kept simple. Just want to make it a hobby? Why not? Homeowners can attach theirs to their homes. If you have kids get them involved as many schools have greenhouses built by elementary and high school students.

Finally, the wholesome taste of a home-grown produce! Everyone knows there is a difference. But really, between you and me it goes beyond just growing. The need to grow is in everyone's blood so with a little bit of perseverance this labor of love will bring forth your passion for life and with the sweet anticipation of 'harvest time' you will understand the sheer pleasure of growing your own.

CHAPTER 2: GREENHOUSE BASICS

Before we start here is a quick review of the basic parts of a greenhouse, how it works and how to maintain the correct environment.

What is a greenhouse?

A greenhouse is also known as a hothouse or glasshouse. It is a place where plants, fruits, vegetables, flowers can be grown all year round. It works by attracting heat from solar radiation which in turn warms the air and soil as well as other components within the greenhouse. The warmed air and soil spurs the growth of plants irrespective of the cooler outdoor temperature.

More in depth details of how a green house functions can be found on line (http://en.wikipedia.org/wiki/Greenhouse).

How does a greenhouse capture heat?

A greenhouse uses glass or polycarbonates that act as a medium to allow sunlight to warm the greenhouse. The greenhouse glass or polycarbonate enclosure traps energy within the structure and the heat in turn provides warmth for the plants and the ground inside. As the sun warms the ground, it continues to radiate heat even after the sun sets.

Venting of the greenhouse is normally done with a small window on the roof of the greenhouse that has a temperature controlled opener so as the window opens the temperature inside drops. This is because of the auto-vent automatic cooling system.

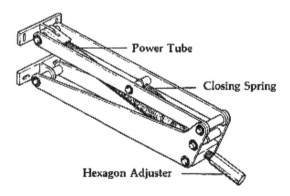

An auto-vent is simply a thermostat used by greenhouses to maintain a desired temperature range. The greenhouse traps the warming effect of sunshine (electromagnetic radiation) and uses the cooling effects of convection to maintain an even temperature. For more in depth details of convection, conduction and radiation review details in Wikipedia (http://en.wikipedia.org/wiki/Greenhouse).

The Greenhouse goes back to the days of the Romans, who as history annals show were the first people to create a structure to protect plants. Using heated pits, they put up slabs of rock to form primitive greenhouses. The term "glasshouse" which is the correct name of this structure, was adopted sometime in the 17th and 18th centuries see reference: Greenhouse History for more details of this history (http://suite101.com/article/history-of-the-greenhouse-a81808)

A common misconception in that era was in believing that heat was more important than light for plants to thrive. Structures were built to exclude the entry of light partly due to the US glass tax of 1845. When this tax was abolished, the design of greenhouses changed to encompass both heat and direct light. As greenhouses evolved, a major change to curved roofs instead of a flat ones, it allowed higher concentrations of the sun's rays. And moving away from the wood structure to iron the greenhouse could be structurally reinforced and made capable of absorbing even more light.

Joseph Paxton, a horticulturist, introduced changes to the greenhouse design using the above concepts. He designed the

Palmhouse at Kew Gardens in the UK which was built in 1842. It measured 360 feet long, 100 feet wide and over 66 feet high. Nine years later, he built the Crystal Palace (made of glass and steel) in Hyde Park, London that provided nearly 1,000,000 sq feet of exhibition space.

Greenhouse design has not changed much in the last forty years except that polycarbonate panels have now in many cases replaced the glass panel. The advantage of the polycarbonate panels is that they are light, have a long life and do not break easily. These improvements in materials have reduced greenhouse costs so that they can be easily and cheaply integrated into any home or business.

The real advantage of having a greenhouse is the capability to extend the growing season. Early vegetables can be planted indoors and then transplanted when they mature. A greenhouse owner also gains several weeks to the growing and sowing period especially if there is a form of heating installed like the use of a Kerosene (aka paraffin) stove or similar.

Being able now to control temperature, light and moisture provides the ideal climate management for most plants; these way consistent results are obtained since most plant varieties enjoy a warm, moist consistent temperature. Stabilizing temperature and moisture inside a greenhouse, you can learn to hone your gardening skills by getting acquainted with as many plant varieties as you can in the greenhouse.

You may want to specialize on one species of fruit, vegetable, flowering plant or fruit tree. Think about it, you can start an orchid in your greenhouse from seed and then transplant them later on into your orchid area. Whatever the intent your greenhouse will give you hours of pleasure. Imagine being able to grow juicy tomatoes or producing new kinds of plants by the simple act of planting from seed.

If space is a problem, there are 'free standing' and 'Lean-to' greenhouses that take just a few square feet of space, and some can be installed on balconies, roof tops, decks and patios.

The choice of greenhouse to suit your needs or 'pocket' can be easily purchased in retail stores as kits or on-line. You can select both type, size and frame color. Frame. If you're not into aluminum, you can build one with a dark frame color or go for earth colors instead.

Summary of the many benefits of the greenhouse:

- control of growing conditions for plants to obtain desired results
- protection from bugs, birds and animals and even the weather

- a means to control pests and diseases
- reduces gardening costs because the owner or gardener grows his own plants
- widens the variety of plants for general gardening
- greenhouses can serve as a means to escape the trial and tribulations of a tough day at work
- good for the soul, relaxes and focuses on the simple pleasure of growing

CHAPTER 3: GREENHOUSE TYPES

There are many different types of greenhouses. The easiest way to decide the type is first of all figure out what you want to grow and how much space you will allocate to your greenhouse My suggestion is to purchase a small unit and experiment for the first year and then finally decide if greenhouse growing is for you. After you decide that you want to build a greenhouse, you should have clear answers to the following questions:

- what will you use your greenhouse for?
- how do I size my greenhouse to meet my needs?
- how much space have can I allocate to my greenhouse?
- what style of greenhouse should I choose; a 'lean-too' or fully framed standalone unit?
- how much am I willing to pay for my greenhouse?

Factors such as cost and space will determine the type of greenhouse you build. If you do live in a windy area, it may be worth to spend the extra money for a solid and sturdy greenhouse. If you are unsure go visit your local hardware store or a nursery, or a do-it-yourself home center, and see the types of models available in your area. Once you decide the greenhouse type you want, check on line to make sure you are getting a good deal.

Here are some typical structural designs to consider;

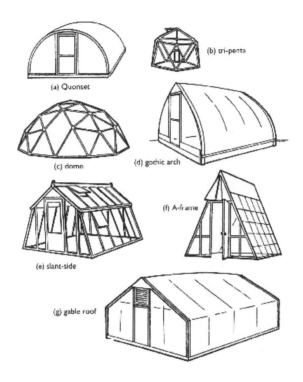

While there may be different types of greenhouse designs, the greenhouse is the same but the designs affect space and temperature.

For example, if temperature is the main factor, because of the plant varieties you want to grow, then there are three types in terms of temperature control. There are also different types of greenhouses based on structural design. We'll start with temperature control factors.

For temperature control purposes, three classifications of greenhouses exist:

- a hot greenhouse
- a warm greenhouse
- a cool greenhouse

I will briefly describe the typical uses of these three types of greenhouses below.

Hot Greenhouse

A hot greenhouse is intended for growing tropical and exotic plants. The inside temperature must be maintained at a minimum of 650F. Heating and lighting will be required particularly if you live in a cold region. Some form of self watering will also be required to maintain ground moisture as well as air humidity necessary for the healthy growth of these exotic plant species.

Warm Greenhouse

A warm greenhouse, sits at about 550F. At this temperature, many varieties of plants can be grown at this temperature as many as you would in your outdoor garden. You will still need to resort to the use of additional heat and light during the winter months if you want to grow year round.

Cool Greenhouse

A cool greenhouse (frost-free greenhouse) must maintain a temperature ranging from 40 to 450F. This temperature is suitable for growing seeds or any plants that do not need warmer temperatures to survive. A cool greenhouse is ideal for starting your plants and vegetables in preparation of the summer months. In most cases the use of heat or lights isn't required for a cool greenhouse unless you live in a very cold climate.

For more in-depth description of greenhouse classification a full review is given at greenhouse types (http://www.articlesbase.com/gardening-articles/16-different-types-of-greenhouse-you-can-use-273391.html). Now that you understand the classes of greenhouses it is now time to briefly review the typical greenhouse structures.

Greenhouse Structures

There are three main types of structure:

- 'lean-to'
- detached
- ridge and furrow or gutter connected.

For detailed descriptions of greenhouse types review the following information found at this site 'greenhouse nursery' (http://aggiehorticulture.tamu.edu/greenhouse/nursery/guides/ghhdbk/struc.html).

'Lean-To'

The 'lean-to' type of greenhouse is rarely used for commercial purposes because of size restrictions, but is the most popular among hobbyists.   The main structure strength comes from the wall that the 'lean-to' is attached to.

Detached

Detached greenhouses, as the name suggests, are independent and are stand alone structures. However, they may still be attached to a work area or else provide access to another greenhouse via a passageway.

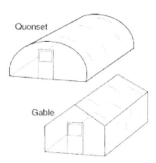

The Quonset is the most common type of detached greenhouse used for commercial production. They are built from arched rafters and have solid walls for support. Quonset greenhouses are ideal for producing most crops, although the growing area is limited to the areas around the side walls, which diminishes efficiency and productivity.

Ridge/Furrow

Ridge and furrow greenhouses are attached at the lower edges of the roof by a gutter. The absence of an inside wall below the gutter allows for increased efficiency. Ridge and furrow greenhouses may be built with gabled or curved arches. Gabled houses are appropriate for heavy coverings (i.e. glass, fiberglass) while curved arch houses are covered with lighter materials (i.e. polyethylene, polycarbonates).

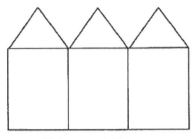

Ridge and Furrow

You may encounter other greenhouse names which are similar to the ones just mentioned above. I've given a brief list of some other typical names. For more in-depth information review the article Greenhouse Construction (http://www.igcusa.com/Technical/greenhouse-types.html)

Cold Frame Type

The roof cover may be poly or shade, end wall covering is either poly or rigid, available lengths come in 12 feet increments, and no gutter connections or vents.

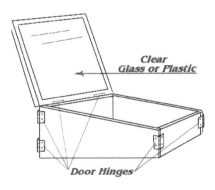

Ground-on-Ground

Roof covering is either poly or shade, wall covering may be poly or rigid, lengths available in 12 feet increments, no gutters, roof vents are available.

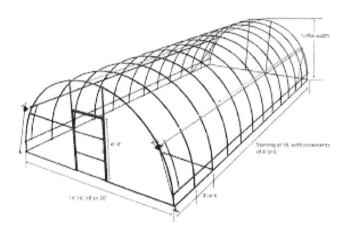

Gutter-connected, Gothic arch

Load rating may be 10, 15 or 20 pounds, roof covering is poly, sidewall and end wall either poly or rigid, lengths available in 12 feet increments while heights available in 8, 10 or 12 feet, gutter connection and roof vents both available.

Gutter-connected Cable

Load rating 10, 20 or 30 pounds, roof covering either poly or rigid, end wall and sidewall covering may be either poly or rigid, lengths in 12 feet increments, gutter connection and roof vents available.

Gutter-connected Arch

Load rating may be 10, 20 or 30 pounds, roof covering and sidewall/end wall is rigid, and lengths come in 12 feet increments, gutter connection and roof vents available.

Glass

Glass type greenhouses are the most traditional covering used. They may be constructed with slanted sides, straight sides and eaves. Aluminum, glass buildings provide low maintenance and have aesthetic lines, as well as ensuring that you get a weather-tight structure. Pre-fabricated glass kits are available for easy installation by hobbyists and amateur gardeners. They come in different models to meet budget and space restrictions. The disadvantages of glass are, its fragile condition (glass breaks easily) and higher costs.

Fiberglass

Fiberglass greenhouses – they are light, strong and hail-proof. Be careful, though, low quality fiberglass will discolor, thus reducing penetration of light. Below is a nice example of a 'lean-to' style greenhouse

Using a good quality fiberglass will however make it as expensive as building a glass one. If you decide to go for fiberglass, go for the most expensive grade, and do not buy colored fiberglass.

Plastic

Plastic greenhouses are becoming very popular for the following reasons:

- Low cost (about 1/6 the cost of glass)
- Absorbs sufficient heat
- Fruits and vegetables and other plants under plastic are comparable in quality to that of glass-grown varieties
- Lower tax liabilities

There are several choices for plastic covering; polyethylene (PE), polyvinyl chloride (PVC), copolymers of these materials and other readily available clear films.

Polyethylene

Polyethylene is lightweight and inexpensive, but tends to deteriorate during the summer when it gets constant exposure to the sun. The deterioration is due to ultraviolet rays and begins along the rafters and along the creases. This problem can be reduced by using UV-inhibited polyethylene, which is available in two and six ml thickness and is up to 40 feet wide and 100 feet long. However in those the northern climates polyethylene tends to do well as it stands up during the seasons of fall, winter and spring.

PVC

Polyvinyl chloride (PVC or Vinyl) - like polyethylene, PVCs are soft and flexible. You can have transparent ones. Vinyl costs two to five times more than polyethylene. When properly installed, they can last as long as five years. Because it attracts dust and dirt from the air, it has to be washed from time to time.

Polycarbonate

Polycarbonate greenhouses are available in a single wall, twin wall or multiwall covering. Polycarbonate is a durable greenhouse glazing material that is virtually unbreakable. Colors of the polycarbonate sheets can be used to create the cool/warm and hot green houses. They are available in clear, white (often called opal) and bronze (often called smoke). Clear is for applications that require maximum light and solar transmission. White is more opaque and is often used in tropical like greenhouses and to hide dirt that may accumulate on the roof or top hide images that are behind the polycarbonate. White also reflects the sun's rays and will not accumulate heat the way bronze can. Bronze will reduce light and heat, but is most often an esthetic choice. Bronze will also expand and contract more, possibly creating noise on large sheets. Read 'Advance Greenhouses' website for more details and examples (http://www.envirocept.com/gh_guide/greenhouse_kits.html).

Greenhouse types are made of many types of material as described above. Each type has its advantages and disadvantages. Whatever you choose make sure you install a stable foundation with a rigid structure suitable for your environment. If in doubt call a professional for advice. However building the greenhouse itself is easy and most people can build it themselves. For more ideas on building greenhouses read the article on greenhouse kits (http://www.envirocept.com/gh_guide/greenhouse_kits.html).

CHAPTER 4: GREENHOUSE PLACEMENT, TOOLS AND MATERIALS

In your greenhouse you can grow just about any type of plant variety, there really are no limitations. Bear in mind, however, that your preference for certain fruits, vegetables and plants will determine the type of greenhouse you should build. 'Know the plant type' is an important factor before deciding on the greenhouse type you will install. Most greenhouses that grow from seed are cool greenhouses that incorporate ventilation to keep air flowing through the greenhouse. However if you decide that your greenhouse is for exotic plants then heat and humidity are essential, thus a hot greenhouse should be used. Note, even with a hot greenhouse there will be a need for ventilation.

Greenhouse Placement

If you have the luxury of a large garden then the ridge of the greenhouse should run east to west - leaving the length of the greenhouse facing the southward sun. Making maximum use of the sun with a south facing aspect will ensure that greenhouse stays warmer than those who do not have this advantage. If you chose to put blinds in your greenhouse at a later stage, which is very simple with a wooden greenhouse, then you need them only for one side. If you are considering a 'Lean-to' greenhouse then a south facing wall is preferred.

You will need a good soil for planting seeds. Compost, potting with moisture control or gardening soil and a little sand or perlite are a good start. As good advice always read all directions in your seed packets as it provides you with all the information you need for this plant type.

Keep some of those black plastic flats that nurseries use to display their plant containers. These are useful for starting seeds and transplants and in essence are free.

Benches in greenhouses are essential, as they hold trays of plants that have already sprouted from seeds and it makes planting less back aching as the planters are at hip height.

Cardboard cups e.g. Jiffy Strips are great for planting seeds or saplings; have several of these trays of cups handy when getting ready to plant.

Seeds sprout quickly and once they grow large enough to move into separate containers, they can be simply transferred into ordinary pots or directly planted into the ground without disturbing the roots since the cups are absorbed in the ground. You can also use yogurt plastic cups, and large commercial type containers that can hold more than one plant. In fact, any container you can think of will be suitable.

Other materials you should have on hand are broken clay pots, cracked walnuts, marbles, charcoal or gravel. These help in proper drainage. Be sure to soak clay pots in water a few minutes before using them. This will prevent the clay from absorbing the moisture from the potting soil.

Backwoodhome provides more details on planting and sewing of seeds (http://www.backwoodshome.com/articles2/sanders67.html).

If you want to have trellises inside your greenhouse, you can make them out of coat hangers which you can bend to any shape you need. Nylon rope is also good for hanging materials as it will not rot.

Herbs are perfect for keeping pests at bay. They are what one writer calls "nature's insecticides". Have a variety of them inside your greenhouse. You can make a natural insecticide by adding onions or garlic to a jar of water. Leave it for a week and spray on your plants.

Other garden tools that will help you run your greenhouse efficiently are air coolers for the hot summer. This is to maintain the temperatures at desired levels. Power vents in the roof are also a good idea to release hot air that can build up suddenly in the summer.

In the winter, a good heater would be nice to warm the greenhouse. Other accessories you need are a humidifier, a CO_2 generator, and a mister.

Further tips on greenhouse growing and when to plant can be found on-line at Greenhouse Tips (http://www.gardeners.com/When-to-Start-Your-Seeds/5215,default,pg.html)

Greenhouse Tables, Shelving and Plant Holders

These are indispensable, especially when you need to work inside your greenhouse and to maximize and organize your greenhouse space. As your plant varieties grow, you will need shelves and tables and plant holders to facilitate your gardening. One popular type of bench that greenhouse hobbyists like is the cedar double layer bench. They are durable and efficient to use. However if space is not an issue, standard metal trellising tables work fine and require zero maintenance.

For shelves, you can opt for two and three section lengths made of aluminum.

Given that watering your plants is an essential – indispensable - part of any greenhouse gardening, a good watering system is required. You can choose either the automatic or hand held watering system to make your watering needs more efficient.

For automatic irrigation systems, there are models that come equipped with an automatic drip irrigation and fertilizer system.

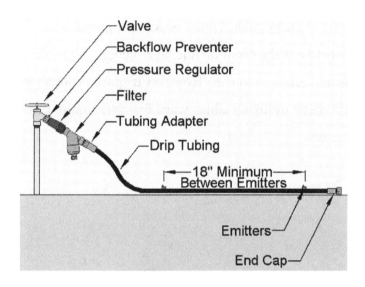

Day or night, they regularly water the plants and adjust the flow of fertilizer. Some have a tank in which the water and fertilizer are mixed and are distributed to plants via hoses, Y-connections and drip pins, see chapter 7 for more details

Greenhouse Lighting System

A type of light called high intensity discharge lighting used to be employed by commercial growers in large greenhouses.

However, the idea of artificial lighting to stimulate plant growth has become very popular. Nowadays most greenhouse businesses are switching to Light Emitting Diodes (LEDs) to stimulate plant growth. The reason being LEDs are extremely cheap to operate as they take a fraction of the power of other equivalent lighting.

LED 'grow-lights' not only adds to natural sunlight, but can actually serve as a substitute during long winters when natural sunlight is limited. Here are just a few of the benefits of LED lighting:

- Stimulates growth and yield rates and increases the health and strength of plants
- Supplements natural sunlight; by using LED lighting, so you can also extend plant 'daylight'

- Enables container outdoor plants on decks and patios during the summer to be moved indoors during the winter

LED lighting is definitely more operationally cost-effective than conventional fluorescents of the same lumens yield but the upfront costs are much higher.   More discussion on this topic can be found at green house tips
(http://www.advancegreenhouses.com/why_use_supplemental_lighting_for%20gree nhouse%20gardening.htm)

Greenhouse Garden Indoor/Outdoor Watering

This is a "self-coiling" garden hose made of rugged and durable polyurethane tubing.   It produces ultra-fine mists and sprays in soft, gentle streams.   Some wand models extend to as long as 50 feet.   No hassle storage because of self-coiling mechanism.

Greenhouse watering systems are constantly evolving in style and design. The current drive is to automate watering based on an electronic timer attached to drip tape hosing. The huge advantage of the automated approach is that you no longer need to remember to water your plants. Additionally you will no longer be held hostage to your plants, so you can take those vacations and know your plants will be fine when you return. Manufacturers are inventing more tools and accessories to make life easier and simpler making our work in greenhouses easier and quicker.

The ones we just described are already being used by many greenhouse enthusiasts. Keep a wary out for new greenhouse inventions as new products will definitely appear in the market place.

Greenhouse Garden Drip Tape Indoor/Outdoor Automated Watering

There are many systems available to automate the process of watering your greenhouse from misters to sprayers to drip tape. The best system on the market is the automated drip tape approach use the easy growing container gardens approach. This book shows step by step the method to automate the watering of all plants in your greenhouse. What is especially advantageous you can grow all your plants directly from compost bags saving you time and backache!

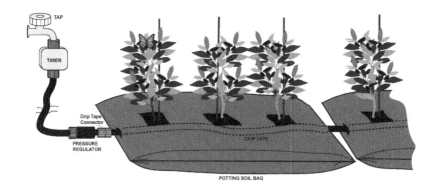

This system can be purchased at the following locations;

- Easygrowing (www.easygrowing.info)
- SandSpublishing (http://sandspublishing.com/wp-store/all-products/easygrowing-container-gardens/)
- Paperback - (http://www.amazon.com/Easy-Growing-Container-Automated-Vegetables/dp/1470051206/)
- Kindle - (http://www.amazon.com/Easy-Growing-Container-Gardens-ebook/dp/B00789FLRS/)
- Nook B&N - (http://www.barnesandnoble.com/w/easy-growing-container-gardens-simon-marlow/1109132324?ean=9781105611223)
- Tablet - Lulu (http://www.lulu.com/shop/simon-marlow/easygrowing-container-gardens-the-automated-container-kitchen-garden-easy-grow-vegetables-flowers/ebook/product-20113265.html)

- iPad/Mac - iBookstore
  (https://itunes.apple.com/us/book/easygrowing-
  container-gardens/id520202515?mt=11)

Use the above links or the search term 'Easygrowing Container Gardens' to find this invaluable resource.

This Page Left Intentionally Blank

Use it for Note Taking

CHAPTER 5: GREENHOUSE GROWING GUIDELINES

If you're growing carrots, beets, turnips and other root crops, they thrive well in deep boxes which can be put under benches. Those that require tub-type containers are tomatoes, peas, cucumbers and pole beans, while lettuce or other low leafy vegetables may be planted in the tub with the taller vegetables. You can plant corn directly on the floor of the greenhouse, in a special bed prepared for it. To save space, you can plant pumpkin between the rows of corn.

Use room temperature water to water your indoor plants. Let tap water stand for a day to get rid of the chlorine substance. This way you avoid your plants getting brown tips. Distribute crushed egg shells in your garden to stimulate growth. Sprinkling coffee grounds will add acid to the greenhouse ground. Before bringing vegetables and fruits from the greenhouse to your house, rinse them well outside; this way dirt and bugs stay outside and will not make your kitchen dirty.

To make more room in your greenhouse, use lower benches for starting seeds and transplants; upper benches for growing flowers and specimen plants. Some vegetables, like tomatoes, should be planted in a warm section of the greenhouse.

Regarding planting of seeds make sure to water lightly for the first few times. Over watering may cause the seeds to come to the surface too soon, preventing them from rooting properly.

Preparation and production must be done in separate areas. Don't do general preparation on the growing floor. This makes for a tidier greenhouse.

Here is a list of the largest vegetables that will need the most spacing in your greenhouse:

- bush type beans: minimum of five feet between rows
- cabbage: a foot between rows
- peppers: about a foot between rows
- cantaloupes: two to three feet between rows
- squash: two to three feet between rows,
- tomatoes and watermelons: minimum of two feet between rows.

All other vegetables (beets, carrots, garlic, lettuce, onions, peas, radishes, spinach, and turnips): five to ten inches to grow fully in the bed in your greenhouse.

For more discussion on the above topics visit the online Advanced Greenhouse (http://www.advancegreenhouses.com) section.

For carrots, beets, and onions that grow deep down in the dirt, keep your soil at least two foot deep as the roots on some of these plants and the vegetable that grows from these plants can get to be very large under the soil.

Mixing vegetables in rows is a good idea. Plants that are different put side by side will not compete for the nutrients, soil and water. For example, take onions and lettuce. One grows down in the dirt while the other grows up from the soil – they grow well side by side. However if you were to put onions and carrots together, they will be competing for the soil space.

Review more on this subject on 'Greenhouse Tips' (http://www.gardeners.com/When-to-Start-Your-Seeds/5215,default,pg.html)

This Page Left Intentionally Blank

Use it for Note Taking

The key to gardening success lies in the soil. Unfortunately, for many of us aspiring green-thumbs, attempting to understand soil can be an overwhelming task; the road to prize winning roses and bumper crops of tomatoes can seem a rocky one at best. However gardeners need not fret. Although soils can be a vast and complicated field of study (that could truly take a lifetime to thoroughly comprehend) the home gardener can achieve great gardening success simply by understanding a few important principles of soil science.

Soil Fertility

First and foremost among these principles is soil fertility. As gardeners, particularly for those of us interested in growing fruits, vegetables, or annual flowers, our successes and failures hinge foremost on the fertility of the soil.

The definition of soil fertility is the ability of a soil to support abundant plant growth (the key word here being abundant). There are two components that contribute to this ability of a soil. The first is that soil contains a sufficient quantity of nutrients. The second is that the nutrients soil contains are available for plants to use. Many of us grasp this first component. We understand that soil needs to contain nutrients to feed plants. There are 16 elements essential to the life of plants. Three of these elements, carbon (C), hydrogen (H), and oxygen (O2), are supplied to plants through the atmosphere. The other 13 essential elements, nitrogen (N), phosphorous (P), potassium (K), calcium (Ca), magnesium (Mg), sulfur (S), iron (Fe), manganese (Mn), zinc (Zn), copper (Cu), boron (B), and molybdenum (Mo), are taken up by plants from the soil through their roots.

We understand this relationship between plants and soil and so we fertilize, but what we don't always take into consideration or perhaps just don't quite appreciate is that soil nutrients need to be in appropriate forms and relative proportions in order to be available for plants to use. This may well explain why some times we achieve great results by adding fertilizer to the garden, while at other times, fertilizing has relatively no effect or even a seemingly negative impact on our plants. There is a reason for this. When it comes to soil, there is always a reason; it's just a matter of getting to the root of it. Developing an understanding of this discrepancy between nutrient quantity and availability can be a huge step in improving the effects of our gardening techniques. The best way grasp this discrepancy is by learning about some other principles of soil and examining how they influence soil fertility, starting with soil texture.

Soil Texture

Soil consists largely of many individual mineral particles. Sand, silt, and clay are the three different types of mineral particles found in soil. Soil texture is a way of describing soils based on their proportions of sand, silt, and clay particles.

Texture has a huge impact on the behavior and characteristics of a soil, heavily influencing both quantity and availability of nutrients. Conveniently enough, soil texture is one of the few soil properties that can easily be determined in the garden through simple observations, which are very worthwhile exercises to practice.

Watching how a garden responds to rainy weather is an excellent indicator of soil texture. Gardens that puddle up and dry out very slowly most likely contain a high proportion of clay, whereas soil that drains freely and dries out quickly probably has a sandy makeup. A better feel for texture can be gotten by taking a sample of soil in your hands. Clay soils work up easily into a ball when moist. They feel rather sticky to the touch, and can be stretched and molded much like modeling clay. Silt soils can also be made into a ball when moist, however, they are not nearly as moldable as clay soils, and have a silky feel to the finger tips. Sandy soils tend to break apart when trying to make into a ball, and have a noticeable gritty feel to the touch. A 'loamy' soil, which has relatively equal proportions of sand, silt, and clay, and is often the desire of most gardeners, will show off all these properties to some extent. It will make a ball that isn't quite as elastic as a clay soil, and will also have a gritty yet silky feel.

A more precise form of in-home analysis of a soils texture can be done by filling a glass jar half full with a sample of soil, then filling the jar the rest of the way with water. The contents are stirred up in the jar and then left to settle apart. Sand particles, being the largest and heaviest will settle out first and fall to the bottom of the jar. Silt particles, being smaller than sand particles, will settle out as the second layer. Lastly the clay particles from the soil sample will settle out as the third layer and rest on top of the silt and sand. When all of the soil particles have settled, the three particle types will have formed three distinguishable bands. Measuring the thickness of each band and dividing it by the overall thickness of the soil sample will give a percentage value for each soil particle. Based on this analysis of soil texture, we can start to predict how our soil is going to behave and make appropriate decisions about management.

Clay Soil

Opposite the large sand particles on the size spectrum are the tiny clay particles. Because they are smaller size, clay particles group much closer together in the soil than sand particles, and therefore the space between particles is much smaller. The small pores between clay particles hold water tightly and restrict the downward movement of water through the soil. This characteristic of clay soils can be beneficial or detrimental. It's helpful that clay soils don't require frequent watering like sandy soils. However, soils with enough clay can almost completely restrict water drainage resulting in a waterlogged garden that can be very damaging to plants. (Fear not though! There are ways of remedying soil texture problems, and we will get to this!)

Sandy Soil

Because sand particles are so large, there are large spaces, or pores, between the individual particles in sandy soils; this allows water to drain readily from the soil and leaves plenty of space for air. This can be advantageous to a gardener because most of the plants we grow don't like sitting in water, and most of the microbial activity beneficial to plants requires an aerobic (oxygen rich) environment. However, sandy soils can also be a problem because they require more frequent watering in dry times, and also lack the ability to store large amounts of nutrients.

What is Cat Ion Exchange Capacity - CEC

In addition to clay's water holding capacity, there is another trait of clay particles that is important to soil fertility. This is the ability of clay to store the nutrients plants need to survive.

Nutrients exist in the soil as cat-ions, tiny atoms with positive electrical charges. In order to be held in the soil, they need to have particles with negative charges that they can bond with; otherwise they are quickly washed out of the soil by rain and irrigation. Due to their chemistry, most clay particles have the necessary negative electrical charge which allows them to attract and store the positively charged plant nutrients. Without going into great detail, these nutrients are then transferred from their hosting site (in this case, a clay particle) to a hungry plant root through water in the soil (and that's how a plant eats, yum).

This ability of soil to store plant nutrients is referred to as a soil's Cat ion Exchange Capacity (CEC). CEC is a measure of the number of negatively charged potential storage sites in a soil. It is another important principle of soil science for gardeners to have an understanding of. The CEC value of a soil is considered a good measurement of potential soil fertility, and clay particles are a key contributor to CEC. More detailed description of CEC and how it works can be found at Gardening Organic (http://www.gardeninginfozone.com/organic)

Organic Matter

Clay particles are not the only particles in the soil that contribute to CEC. Organic matter, more specifically humus particles, also offer negatively charged sites that can store plant nutrients in the soil. Organic matter (OM) is the term used to describe the plant and animal derived components of soil. There are many different sources of OM and they exist in many different forms. Leaves, wood chips, manure, weeds (also known as green manure) are just a few. Microorganisms in the soil feed on OM, breaking it down to smaller and smaller particles. The final destination of OM is humus, a small, stable, negatively charged particle that has a high water and nutrient storing capacity. Thus humus also contributes to a soil's CEC. Generally speaking, a soil with a high clay content and large amounts of OM will have a high CEC, while sandy soils with little OM have low CEC's. This is an important distinction to make about our soil, as the two soil types need to be managed very differently.

Since soils with low CEC's can only hold limited amounts of nutrients, fertilizing applications should be kept to small quantities because any added nutrients that cannot be held in the soil will quickly wash down through the soil. This downward movement of excess nutrients through soil is called leaching and it can be a contributing factor in water pollution. (Not to mention a waste of money!)

Much like how soils at either end of the texture spectrum (clay-sand) can be advantageous or disadvantageous for a gardener, CEC at either range of the spectrum can be beneficial or problematic given the specific circumstance. Soils with a high

CEC (keep in mind if your soil has a high clay content and lot's of organic matter it will have a high CEC) offer the obvious of advantage of being able to store lot's of nutrients. However, because these soils hold larger quantities of nutrients when imbalances occur they require larger amounts of amendments to correct than soils with low CEC's that have similar imbalances.

Cat Ion Exchange Capacity and Soil pH

Soils are not selective about what they store. They can potentially store cat ions that are not plant nutrients, which can negatively affect plant health. Two examples of cat ions that compete for storage space with plant nutrients and that have an important impact of plants are Hydrogen (H) and Aluminum (Al). Hydrogen contributes to the pH level of a soil. The more H present in the soil the lower the pH (which means the soil is more acidic). Soil pH is important to manage because it influences soil chemistry, altering the forms at which certain nutrients exist.

At very low pH levels, many of the essential plant nutrients become less available to plants, while other potentially toxic elements become more available. Aluminum is an excellent example of the latter case. It can be very toxic to plants', however it is only present in the soil in a form that can be threatening at pH levels below 5.0.

Most of the crops we grow as gardeners do best in soil with a pH level between 6.0 and 7.0, the range at which nutrients are most available to plants. Maintaining a pH level within this range is critical to maintaining soil fertility. Low pH levels can be raised by using lime or lowered by adding garden sulfur, an acidifying amendment. Keep in mind, soils with a high CEC require larger amounts of material to raise or lower their pH level than soils with a low CEC because they are storing more acidity (more Hydrogen cat ions). The advantage of these soils is that they are buffered better against unwanted pH changes. See 'Soil pH' for more on this subject (http:// www.comfylawn.com).

The Right Balance:

Often times a soil can be in our ideal pH range and have sufficient nutrients, but some nutrients are present in proportions that are interfering with the availability of other essential nutrients. In effect, nutrients are competing with one another. In these instances, soil fertility requires bringing balance to the nutrient levels in the soil. This is where a soil test can be a very helpful tool.

There are a number of reputable institutions that can provide this relatively inexpensive analysis of your soil. Search the internet to find a local test provider. The tests offer a detailed description of specific soil nutrient levels in your soil based on laboratory tests.

With this tool in hand, you can see which nutrient levels are low, perhaps limiting plant growth, or which nutrients are present in such high levels that they are out-competing other nutrients. When imbalances are present, high CEC soils will require larger amounts of amendments than low CEC soil, but once corrected, balanced nutrient levels will be easier to maintain.

The Appliance of Science; Putting it all together

Now that you have gained an appreciation of some principles of soil science and understand how they contribute to soil fertility, you can make calculated decisions about how to improve your gardens. For example, you can now identify that you have a sandy soil which is why your plants always seem to be struggling. Applying the knowledge of soil science, you can choose to add some organic matter to your soil to improve water and nutrient storage capacity. If you determine that your sandy soil also needs a nutrient boost, you know to apply fertilizer in small doses (because sandy soils have low CEC) so as not to lose fertilizer to leaching.

If on the other hand your plants are drowning in a clay soil, you know soil fertility hinges on improving drainage. You can do this by applying organic matter to increase airspace in the soil. Or you could use gypsum a particularly good amendment for improving the water problems of clay soil. While it might seem logical to add sand to a clay soil, sand in some cases when mixed with clay can create an almost concrete like soil structure. Refer to 'Soil Structure' (http://www.naturalengland.org.uk/Images/EA-think-soils_tcm6-28196.pdf) for more details.

When your garden dilemma is not a simple a soil texture issue (say you have a loamy soil with lots of organic matter, but plants are still struggling) by drawing on your knowledge of the soil's inner workings you can deduce that your problem is related to a pH or nutrient imbalance. By having your soil tested, you can determine the specific problem and then choose the appropriate fertilizer to remedy the imbalance.

Even in those utterly frustrating instances when soil texture is fine and tests show a pH and nutrient balance, but plants still struggle and insects and diseases run rampant, you can take a moment. Stop and consult your knowledge of soil science, put your trust in that knowledge, and hold off on the use of potentially unnecessary pesticides or fertilizers. Sometimes plants may be struggling simply because your soil doesn't have enough organic matter to support healthy microbial populations. These helpful microbes rely on organic matter in the soil as a food source. When present they form symbiotic relationships (good partnerships) with plants. These mutually beneficial relationships between plants and microbes that can be all the difference between healthy thriving plants able to fend of insect and disease pests, and struggling plants that act like beacons to insects and diseases looking for weak prey (the importance of Organic Matter can't be emphasized enough).

Understanding a few principles of the fascinating science of soil can take a lot of the mystery and guess work out of gardening. Furthermore, it can make our lofty ambitions of blue ribbons and bumper crops achievable. And last but not least, by gaining an understanding and appreciation of soil and applying our knowledge in our gardens we can each in our own little way contribute to improving the health of our environment. As gardeners we all have the potential to be more than just weekend warriors, with study, practice, and care we can be stewards of sustainability. As such each time we walk away from an afternoons work in the garden, we can sit back knowing then we have not only done a little to feed ourselves and our families, but that we have also done our part to care for our earth.

Chapter 7: Greenhouse Watering and Water Conservation

The Drip Irrigation approach is the ultimate in water conservation. If you want to find out more about using drip irrigation check out this book on drip irrigation (http://www.simplybetterway.com/blog/greensherpa-store/). Use the system and you will not only be helping save hundreds of dollars on your water bill but also help save the precious water we have on this planet. Only 1% of the world's water supply is drinkable, this number is shrinking and the planet populace is expanding. Now is the time that YOU can help the planet. I've added a few more tips in this section for your interest and added a section at the end that shows the breakdown of water usage in the US as recorded by the US Geological Survey (http://ga.water.usgs.gov/edu/wateruse.html It will open your eyes!

Greenhouse Watering

Whether you have a hot, warm or cool green house you need to regularly water your plants. This tends to be time consuming and water wasteful as plants need to be watered regularly with just the right amount of water to keep the soil moist. This is true for vegetables, flowers and other plant types. Watering with a watering can or hose will result in uneven and wasteful watering. Putting in a drip system will benefit both you and your plants because;

- watering is automated and so frees you to do other stuff
- keeps your plants evenly watered and waters at the optimum time of day

Early morning is generally better than dusk preventing the growth of fungus. Early watering, and late watering, also reduce water loss to evaporation. Watering early in the day is also the best defense against slugs and other garden pests. Try not to water when it's windy - wind can blow sprinklers off target and speed evaporation.

Add Organic Matter

Adding organic material to your soil will help increase its absorption and water retention. Areas which are already planted can be 'top dressed' with compost or organic matter. Use an 'Earth Machine', a simple composter that decomposes all your vegetable waste, grass and leaves. Requires NO intervention from YOU other than adding your waste! This can be used to fertilize all your plants

Water Your Lawn Only When It Needs It.

A good way to see if your lawn needs watering is to step on the grass. If it springs back up when you move, it doesn't need water. If it stays flat, the lawn is ready for watering. Letting the grass grow taller (to 3") will also promote water retention in the soil. Deep-soak your lawn long enough for the moisture to soak down to the roots where it will do the most good. A light sprinkling can evaporate quickly and tends to encourage shallow root systems. Put an empty tuna can on your lawn - when it's full, you've watered about the right amount. Doing this means you cut the grass less so less CO_2 into the environment and more leisure time for you. Oh and by the way if you do feed your lawn do it in the fall not the spring unless you want to spend more time cutting your grass!

Use Efficient Watering Systems For Shrubs, Flower Beds And Lawns.

You can greatly reduce the amount of water used for shrubs, beds and lawns with strategic placement of drip-irrigation systems (http://eartheasy.com/grow_drip-irrigation.htm), soaker hoses and rain barrel water catchment systems (http://eartheasy.com/water-conservation). A watering meter can be easily added to your hose to monitor water usage to required needs. Avoid over-watering plants and shrubs, as this can actually diminish plant health and cause yellowing of the leaves. For long-term water savings, consider adding moisture-retaining lassenite to your lawn and shrub beds.

Plant Drought-Resistant Shrubs And Plants

Many beautiful shrubs and plants thrive with far less watering than other species. Replace herbaceous perennial borders with native plants. Native plants will use less water and be more resistant to local plant diseases.   Plant slopes with plants that will retain water and help reduce runoff.

Put A Layer Of Mulch Around Trees And Plants

Mulch will slow evaporation of moisture while discouraging weed growth. Adding 2 - 4 inches of organic material such as compost or bark mulch will increase the ability of the soil to retain moisture.

Don't Water The Pavement Or Sidewalk

Position your sprinklers so water lands on the lawn or garden, not on paved areas. Also, avoid watering on windy days.

Don't Run The Hose While Washing Your Car

Clean the car using a pail of soapy water. Use the hose only for rinsing - this simple practice can save as much as 150 gallons when washing a car. Use a spray nozzle when rinsing for more efficient use of water. Better yet, use a waterless car washing system; there are several brands, such as EcoTouch, which are now on the market.

- Use a broom, not a hose, to clean driveways and sidewalks
- Use a broom or blower to keep the sidewalks and driveways clear.

Check For Leaks In Pipes, Hoses, Faucets And Couplings

Leaks outside the house may not seem as bad since they're not as visible. But they can be just as wasteful as leaks indoors. Check frequently to keep them drip-free. Use hose washers at spigots and hose connections to eliminate leaks. Use timers to water your garden so you don't forget to put the hose off!

Water conservation comes naturally when everyone in the family is aware of its importance, and parents take the time to teach children some of the simple water-saving methods around the home which can make a big difference

Water usage as recorded by the US Geological Society. [1] This is worth going to this site and just see how the US uses its precious water, excellent site and articles.

This Page Left Intentionally Blank

Use it for Note Taking

CHAPTER 8: BRING LIFE TO YOUR GREENHOUSE

The fun of growing your own plants is that you become the plant's custodian. You by working soil with seed will bring to life your very own creation. You can grow just about anything you like. It is an oasis for restoring sanity to an already crazy world. The time that you spend tending to your greenhouse can be your downtime, a time away where the stresses of this world pass away leaving you with the simple task of growing, a time honored profession from our ancestors. If your greenhouse is your hobby, you will wish to spend allotted time there each and every day. If you want to understand how to survive should a world catastrophe occur you will be well prepared to sustain yourself, your family and your community. If however you just want to consider your greenhouse as a means to growing fresh food, you will go back to nature and get in touch with your organic self. All of this is very good for well being.

Four Personal Reasons for Purchasing a Greenhouse

Achieve peace of mind and gain the ancient art of growing from seed. Your greenhouse can be attached to your home. It can alternatively be freestanding to add to the beauty of your surrounding landscape. If you are an avid gardener then you will likely enjoy the atmosphere of a greenhouse. You do not need a large commercial greenhouse to be successful. A small greenhouse will provide you the warmth and ambience of your own personal space. You will have a greenhouse on a much smaller scale, a place to house your personal choices in plants, flowers and fruits and vegetables. You will also have a very handy place to do the work you need to do without being interrupted. You will be in your own domain and not under someone else's green thumb.

Develop a hobby that can become a business. Owning your own greenhouse sure saves you a bundle when it comes time for buying seeds. You can capture your own seeds from your garden and then transfer those to your greenhouse. This saves money during the springtime.

As you spend more time with your greenhouse, you will be amazed by how many seeds you can start there. You will learn more about growing and rely less and less on the commercial growers! In no time at all, your greenhouse will begin to pay for itself.

When you own your own greenhouse, you will have the opportunity to expand it as just a hobby. You can become equipped to grow flowers, vegetables and plants all through the year. Having your own greenhouse means you can be free of growing just for spring growing seasons. You can grow throughout the entire year. This is true even if you do not wish for the expenses of heating throughout the winter months.

Begin by planting seeds, March through April and then plan to plant again, May through June. During the cooler temperatures, place your plants in the greenhouse. This will mean a much longer life span for your flowers and vegetables.

Develop a healthy organic mindset.   Another good reason for owning a greenhouse is that you can plant and harvest your own organic foods, vegetables, fruits, and herbs. This will save on your grocery bills and will also make for very healthy eating. Those with food allergies and chemical sensitivities prefer to eat organic foods and this makes owning a greenhouse ideal for them.

Share the knowledge and teach your family the art of growing. Owning a greenhouse is pure pleasure for the entire family. Each member can have their own little organic corner where they are in control. Watching a plant begin from seed and then grow into plants is a delight.

From Little to Bountiful

Your greenhouse has so much to offer you. Have you ever taken the time to think about all of the plenty that your greenhouse does offer you?

When you take a walk through the front door of your imagined greenhouse, what do you see? Your every sense will come alive with color, scent and sight! You will feel alive in every sense of the word. Everywhere there will be new growth! It is pure delight! If you are ever feeling homebound, just peek you head inside your greenhouse for an instant boost of pure energy.

As you return to your hobby greenhouse, you have the pleasure of knowing that your tomatoes life span will continue into the fall. By the time the Christmas holidays come along, you will have ripe and fresh tomatoes to enjoy.

You will save money by buying your seeds in bulk from catalogs or, perhaps, by trading seeds with friendly gardeners for free. You can next start your flowers and plants come January. You will feel like quite the garden manager!

You spend so many hours at work and running to meet the needs of others that when you spend a little time doing something that you really enjoy you feel more worthwhile inside. You can start and grow trees and shrubs without the worry of deer and other animals coming and eating them when they are small and vulnerable. Starting and keeping your trees and shrubs indoors for a year will give them an extra edge so they can grow larger and stronger before being faced by animals.

If you want to be on your own, away from the clatter of life, you can simply walk down the aisles of your greenhouse and reflect on your day. All around you are the great creations of nature that you had a hand in yourself! This is very nourishing to the spirit and helps you to gather your thoughts in a positive reflection.

If you are a mother, you can bring your children to the greenhouse and teach them the lessons of the earth. They can get your hands dirty with Mother Nature and then watch as their plants grow and flourish!

You can start to grow early on and watch the beauty of your own bounty before all of those who do not have a greenhouse. You will enjoy your spring flowers and vegetables early!

Your neighbors and your friends might watch you and wish that they, too, had a terrific greenhouse! As you tend to your plants year round, you feel fulfilled inside, as you are doing something that is very important. Helping to bring wholesome and natural foods to your family's table each day brings its own reward!

You spend so much time each day running here and there and always doing for others, with your own greenhouse, what you do there is for you and for those you choose to share your bounty. This brings a sense of satisfaction.

Make Money To Cover Your Costs

The amount of vegetables and flowers that you grow in your greenhouse will always over exceed your needs. There are two great ways to make this excessive bounty to your advantage;

- Sell your excess in from stalls or local farmers markets
- Freeze those vegetables for a later winter snack and get the great taste of summer all year long

Owning a personal greenhouse brings with it many rewards – perhaps the most important being the feeling of extreme accomplishment that comes from all of the hard work you do there. It is time very well spent and enjoyed!

CHAPTER 9: GREENHOUSE LOVERS / HOBBYISTS
ADDITIONAL RESOURCES

This chapter provides sources of information on greenhouses and other related topics. There are on-line web sources and on line ebooks on the subject

For readers interested in what the government's position is on greenhouses – soil, emissions, nurseries, tomatoes, etc visit the United States Department of Agriculture web site (http://www.usda.gov/wps/portal/usda/usdahome)

This link takes you directly to the subject of USDA major topics including greenhouses.

For more greenhouse tips covering topics such as: humidity, strawberry tips, opening a greenhouse business, fall greenhouse tips, hanging baskets in the greenhouse, visit the online site (http://www.greenhouses.com/)

If you want to learn how to build your own greenhouse, and want to have as many possible plans to choose from, visit the website (http://www.floridagardener.com). In the 'Growing Tips' menu select 'Build a Greenhouse'. This site has some illustration plans with step-by-step instructions on building a custom greenhouse.

For subjects covering:

- Choosing Your Greenhouse
- Choosing a Greenhouse Site
- Foundation Hints
- Frequently Asked Questions
- Seeds in the Spring

Visit the website (http://www.gardenstyles.com)

For further references on education there are many good sites that provide accurate and updated information. A few of these are;

- To teach students about greenhouses using a broad and general approach; (http://www.climatechange.gc.ca)
- To show children how the greenhouse effect would contribute to global warming, through animation, (http://www.epa.gov/globalwarming/kids)
- For greenhouse beginners, this book provides a more thorough in depth description of the basics for specialty plants. The title of the book in paperback is; 'In Your Greenhouse: A Beginner's Guide' by Greta Heinen. How enjoying outdoor gardening with specialty plants can lead one to consider a hobby greenhouse.

- Another recommended paperback book is: 'Greenhouse Gardener's Companion: Growing Food and Flowers in Your Greenhouse or Sunspace' by Shane Smith, Marjorie C. Leggitt is the illustrator. Thos book covers the topics of; building your own greenhouse, do it yourself glazing, optimizing the greenhouse interior design and watering concepts

No matter what you decide I recommend you start with a low cost investment. Start a simple 'cold frame' and see what works for you before you invest in a large greenhouse.

This Page Left Intentionally Blank

Use it for Note Taking

CHAPTER 10: CHECKLIST FOR BUYING A GREENHOUSE

Structure or Framework

- Aluminum - wood if beautiful, but our aluminum frames are longer lasting and maintenance-free.
- Painted Aluminum - best appearance, looks new for many years.

Glazing or Polycarbonate

- Tempered safety glass
- Twin Wall or Opal
- Triple Wall
- Glass walls, Twin Wall or Opal roof

See more details on polycarbonate greenhouses at 'Advance Greenhouses'
(http://www.advancegreenhouses.com/polycarbonate_greenhouses.htm)

Foundation types

- Pressure treated timbers (up to 200 sq ft greenhouse)
- Concrete/block base wall, up to 9inches above slab
- Concrete slab/tile not too smooth or it gets slippery. You also should consider drainage!

Floor

If you have not poured a concrete slab, you will need a walkway down the middle of your greenhouse. First, lay down landscape fabric over the entire floor. For an aisle of bricks: frame the walkway with treated 2 x 4 lumber, lay down 2" of crushed rock, then 1" of sand, and set the bricks with 3/8" spacing. A final touch might be to plant lemon thyme between the bricks! Finish the remainder of the floor with 2" of gravel using pea or any other crushed stone.

Accessories

- Benches
- Air Circulation wall ports and roof openers
- Watering system, preferably drip tape

CHAPTER 11: CONCLUDING THOUGHTS

There's something about a seed that mystifies and stimulates human imagination; seeing life take shape from seed to mature plant. But the real secret of the greenhouse is about self-sufficiency, good nutrition and well being.

Many centuries ago, greenhouses were the monopoly of the rich European and American aristocrats. At that time, only the rich were able to import rare and exotic plants from foreign countries and had the resources to build expensive structures in which to store these exotic plants. Happily that monopoly turned into a commodity that the ordinary person can now afford. As styles and designs quickly evolved, greenhouses became within the reach of the small scale entrepreneur

Greenhouses not only became plant protectors, cultivators and all-season sanctuaries for growing plants, but also a refuge for the weary and a business for the amateur and expert horticulturists. The greenhouse is a welcome escape from the urban decay that characterizes cities in transition. Once you've tasted fresh, juicy tomatoes or rich red sweet strawberries 'harvested' in the greenhouse, you will shun the bland supermarket varieties that pale in comparison with greenhouse ripened vegetables.

In reflection growing plants in your very own greenhouse will elevate you to the levels of the great and might. Take Joseph Paxton for example, he built the Crystal Palace in England, a very large greenhouse that has been acclaimed by many as a piece of architectural art that is unsurpassed to date. It was as long as eighteen soccer fields and as wide as eight. But in real life he was a gardener for large estates and this is where he designed many of the modern day glass greenhouses.

It was told that Joseph Paxton built a specific green house for one plant known as the giant Victoria Regia lily for the specific purpose of providing a supply of these lilies to the Duke of England, a flower the duke wanted to bestow upon the current Queen, Queen Victoria.

Imagine the recognition Joseph Paxton received! Not only did Paxton manage to grow the lily he actually managed to get 126 blooms from his plants.

Now I'm not saying that having your own greenhouse will make you famous but you in fact tread the ground of the rich and famous just by the sheer act of growing your own plants. Think about this, find plants that are difficult to grow, become an expert in growing them and just watch your reputation take-off in a good way. However most importantly, owning a greenhouse will make you appreciate the meaning of life by bringing you closer to the soil that nurtures the food that keeps you alive.

A last word on greenhouse gardening. Much as it stimulates a passion in all of us to grow plants it can also be time consuming and ritualistic. You need to be around at certain times to care for your plants. It is important to understand this before investing heavily into your 'dream' greenhouse. I heavily suggest you start with a low cost investment like using 'cold-frames' to grow a selection of plants including herbs, tomatoes and beans. This will give you an idea of the level of commitment required to grow your own produce and to see if it fits in with your lifestyle. This low cost approach will provide you with all the challenges of growing without the risk of a high investment and if you find that growing is not for you then your investment risk is low allowing you to walk away without losing your shirt.

As ever I would not leave such an important topic on a negative note. Growing plants is an age old tradition that has taken the human race from survival of the fittest to the vast civilizations now that inherit the earth. In the development of our species we are beginning to lose our link with nature. This is dangerous as we all assume that the human race will continue to grow and develop. However if for some reason we meet with a catastrophic event those that can grow plants are more likely to survive than those who have are sustained on processed food. So here is your chance get your thumbs green and learn to grow just about anything. Have fun!

EXTEND YOUR KNOWLEDGE

EasyGrowing Container Gardens - The Automated Container Kitchen Garden Easy Grow Vegetables & Flowers

Discover how to build a fully automated plant, vegetable and flower growing system. This book and guide will lead you through the complete process of purchasing, setting up and maintaining your easy grow container garden. There are some small initial purchases required but after that all the equipment used is re-usable year after year. The only things that require annual replacement are the compost bags which you can purchase at any of the large home garden retailers (compost bags with moisture control). The secrets to growing plants and vegetables on auto-pilot requires neither specialist skills nor a natural green thumb. This system is so easy you will be amazed at how successful you become in growing great plants and succulent vegetables with little to no effort. The Automated Kitchen Container Garden grows abundant succulent vegetables and colorful plants. This step by step guide shows you how to achieve great results:

No Manual Watering, No Weeding, No Feeding and No Effort Just Happy Growing!

WWW.EASYGROWING.INFO

The Growers Handbook of Planting All Types of Plants

REFERENCES

http://en.wikipedia.org/wiki/Greenhouse

http://suite101.com/article/history-of-the-greenhouse-a81808

http://www.articlesbase.com/gardening-articles/16-different-types-of-greenhouse-you-can-use-273391.html

http://aggiehorticulture.tamu.edu/greenhouse/nursery/guides/ghhdbk/struc.html

http://www.igcusa.com/Technical/greenhouse-types.html

http://www.envirocept.com/gh_guide/greenhouse_kits.html

http://www.backwoodshome.com/articles2/sanders67.html

http://www.advancegreenhouses.com/why_use_supplemental_lighting_for%20greenhouse%20gardening.htm

http://www.gardeninginfozone.com/organic

http:// www.comfylawn.com

http:// www.capecodgroundwater.org)

http://ga.water.usgs.gov/edu/wateruse.html

http://eartheasy.com/grow_drip-irrigation.htm

http://eartheasy.com/water-conservation

http://www.advancegreenhouses.com/polycarbonate_greenhou
ses.htm

http://www.naturalengland.org.uk/Images/EA-think-
soils_tcm6-28196.pdf

CPSIA information can be obtained at www.ICGtesting.com
Printed in the USA
LVOW04s1826140914

404006LV00024B/827/P